Genetics and Human Behavior

Genetics and Human Behavior

Ronnee Yashon and Michael R. Cummings

MOMENTUM PRESS
HEALTH

MOMENTUM PRESS, LLC, NEW YORK

Genetics and Human Behavior

Copyright © Momentum Press, LLC, 2020.

First published in 2020 by
Momentum Press, LLC
222 East 46th Street, New York, NY 10017
www.momentumpress.net

ISBN-13: 978-1-94664-648-4 (paperback)
ISBN-13: 978-1-94664-649-1 (e-book)

Momentum Press Human Genetics and Society Collection

Cover and interior design by Exeter Premedia Services Private Ltd., Chennai, India

First edition: 2020

10 9 8 7 6 5 4 3 2 1

Printed in the United States of America.

Abstract

This book will look at behavior in a different way. Have you heard of the phrase *nature is nurture*? Simply, it asks what influences our behavior? This has been a debated topic since early man. *Nature* is usually defined as what is given to us before we are born, specifically, in this book, genetics. *Nurture* means learning that we acquire from our environment (parents, friends, and other influences). In this book, we will look at the newest scientific work, how both genetics and environment effect how we behave. Our court system is slowly changing, as science rears its head in the area of criminal law, everyday life, public opinion, and politics.

Keywords

behavior; central nervous system; brain; peripheral nervous system; neurotransmitters; chromosomes; synapse; twin studies; monozygotic; heterozygotic; twin studies; epigenetics; acetylcholine; dopamine; norepinephrine; serotonin; endorphin; single gene defect

Contents

Preface ix

Chapter 1   Behavior 1

Chapter 2   Physiology 1 3

Chapter 3   Physiology 2 7

Chapter 4   Neurotransmitters 9

Chapter 5   How Might Genetics Change Behavior? 13

Chapter 6   Does Any Single Gene Defect (Mutation) Cause
Aggressiveness? 17

Chapter 7   How Do We Study the Effects of Genetics on Behavior? ... 21

Chapter 8   Twin Studies 25

Chapter 9   Legal and Ethical Questions 29

Chapter 10   Famous or Infamous Cases 33

Bibliography 37

About the Authors 39

Index 41

Preface

This book will look at behavior in a different way. Have you heard of the phrase *nature versus nurture*? Simply, it asks what influences our behavior? This has been a debated topic since early man. *Nature* is usually defined as what is given to us before we are born, specifically, in this book, genetics. *Nurture* means learning that, is acquired from our environment (parents, friends, and other influences). In Addition, we will look at the newest scientific work, how both genetics and environment effect how we behave. Our court system is slowly changing, as science rears its head in the area of criminal law, everyday life, public opinion, and politics (Table P.1).

Table P.1 Are these nature and nurture? Or both?

Right or left handedness?	Even though this is known to be genetic, it can be changed by training.	A number of years ago, teachers were told not to allow lefties to use their dominant hand.
Violent personality?	Brain chemicals and hormones control this.	A tie-in to violence has influenced by brain chemical.
Athletic prowess?	Certain traits (height, muscularity) can be enhanced by drugs and other stimulants.	Can someone short be a great basketball player?
Color blindness?	Nature	Always genetic or cannot be cured or changed, except for contact lenses.
Sleepwalking?	No	Usually triggered by stress.
Intelligence?	There are theories (eugenics).	Robert Clark Graham began a sperm bank he called the Repository for germinal choice, also known as genius sperm bank.

CHAPTER 1

Behavior

Simply, behavior can be defined as a reaction to a stimulus; this sounds pretty silly, because if we look at one stimulus, it can have many reactions among many people. The stimulus might be a loud sound or a complicated thought.

Scientists studied the behavior of animals and wondered why they do certain actions. One of the early animal behaviorists (Pavlov) studied what dogs can learn. Since then, animal behavior is still studied, but with an eye to comparing it with humans.

If you watch an animal (say a dog), you will see it learns new behaviors if rewarded (usually with food). But then, so do humans; advertising is an example.

Lets do a small experiment. A few years ago, a very famous actress said she would like to see Orangutans in the wild.

First they took her to an area where baby orangutans were brought when their mothers were killed.

These babies were so very cute, they climbed all over her and she laughed and laughed even when one peed on her.

After, she said she would like to see a grown male.

Because the males live a solitary life, she sat on the road waiting. All the photographers hid.

He came out on the road (see figure 1.1) and moved toward her. She stayed perfectly still as he moved toward her. He reached out his hand and touched her (she was calm), then hugged her!

The photographers ran out to pull him off her but she was calm, and so was she. What was the reason for the hug?

Does animal behavior predict what behavior humans might have?

The answer is *probably*. So, why are we testing on animals first?

Because we do not want to test on people, possibly because of any number of consequences, such as: side effects, lawsuits, mistakes, bad publicity, and of course, loss of revenue.

But, if you look at animals versus humans in drug testing, you can see how dangerous it can be for drug companies to skip the animal trial if something would go wrong when humans are using it.

Note: Why this is important in courts:

As humans, we feel in control of our actions, so if we lose control, we might feel angry, guilty, sorry, or happy.

CHAPTER 2

Physiology 1

In humans, behavior is controlled by the brain and spinal cord. Reflexes are a perfect example. They react quickly and protect us from more harm.

OUR FIRST BEHAVIORAL MULTIPLE CHOICE QUESTION

You walk into the kitchen and a pot is boiling over on the stove. What do you do?

> a. *Ask someone*
> b. *Look for clues (burner on, smell of food)*
> c. *Touch the pot to see if it is hot*
> d. *Walk away*

Answer: All of these might be correct, and your response may change because of your age, previous knowledge, and the word hot! If you choose c, you might be hurt, or your reflexes might kick in (see Figure 2.1).

Most of our behaviors begin with a stimulus traveling to the brain *first*, but not reflexes. Your reflexes tell your body, *danger!* The stimulus then goes to the spinal cord, which immediately sends a message to the arm muscle to contract and pull your hand away. It bypasses the brain and solves the immediate problem. Because nothing is perfect, you might still get a burn, but not as severe. Our brain will store this reflex. See Illustration 2.1.

There are two types of reflexes: the autonomic reflex, affecting inner organs, and the somatic reflex, affecting muscles.

Other reflexes: blinking, pupil opening and closing (in response to light), arm or leg responding to a pin prick (in response to pain), coughing or sneezing (response to irritants or allergens in the nasal cavity), and knee jerk (response to a blow to the knee).

Other brain functions are routed through different areas of the brain (see Illustration 2.3). Sight is a good example. When light enters the eye, it is turned into electrical impulses by passing through the retina. These impulses travel up the optic nerve into the spinal column and up to the brain.

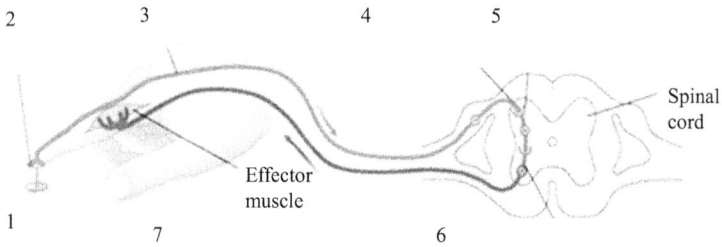

Figure 2.1 Reflex arc

Reflex

Reflex arch: A reflex arc is a neural pathway that controls a reflex. In vertebrates, most sensory nerves do not pass directly into the brain, but synapse in the spinal cord. Follow the steps in the following figure:

1 and 2: Stimulus (heat, injury, or pain)

3 and 4: Carrying the impulse to the spinal cord

5 and 6: Impulse enters the spinal cord and immediately leaves, carrying the impulse to the muscle

7: Muscle that is stimulated moves the finger away

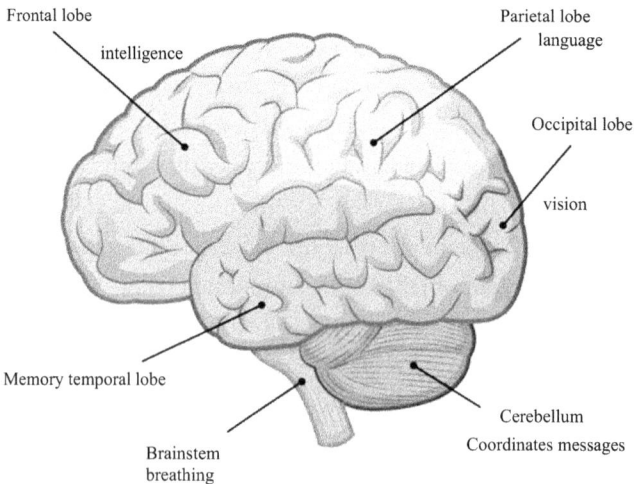

Figure 2.2 Human brain

Areas of the Human brain

In our example, the impulses are sent to the area of the brain that controls sight (see Figure 2.2) and the impulses are read. Then, they are converted back into impulses and sent to the eye, and this is what our brain identifies as an image.

Think about how long it takes to notice something, look at it, and, identify it. It happens almost immediately, and you see what your eyes were sending to the brain.

You see it, and then, you immediately remember you have seen it before.

What if it is something you have never seen before? Your brain might identify it as a familiar sight. But, if you do not identify it, you will be able to find something close to it, and our brain takes over to give you the answer.

This is just one of the amazing things that the brain does: It also stores information, makes information available to you, and controls your emotions and behaviors. *All in a split second.*

Many things can go wrong with impulses moving through the peripheral nerves to the brain. If a person loses a neural connection, the optic (eye) center does not get the message. This can lead to temporary or permanent blindness.

Scientists usually separate behaviors into innate behaviors (present at birth) and learned behaviors (behavior that is acquired through experience, observation, and teaching).

These two types of behaviors can also be called *nature versus nurture* (see Chapter 1). In this book, we will be looking at both sides of this argument.

Is this "really" an argument?

Short example: Much of what we will cover in this book is determining which behavior leads to an action and is this action reasonable. If you are mad at someone, you might slap them. What causes this behavior? Was it automatic? On purpose? Because of something he or she said or did?

The legal system tries to understand motivation, but sometimes cannot clearly define it.

Example: Premeditation? An accident? Or insanity?

BEHAVIORAL MULTIPLE CHOICE QUESTION 2:

You are on a jury, the crime is murder, the suspect says
he was sleep walking and was not responsible.
How do you vote?

a. *Not guilty, because he could not control what he did.*
b. *Guilty, because sleep walking is not a defense.*
c. *Not guilty, because he was not aware of what he was doing.*
d. *Trial is suspended because the judge does not understand the evidence (science?)*

CHAPTER 3

Physiology 2

The areas of the central nervous system (CNS) that control our behavior are the *brain* and *spinal cord*.

Second, the peripheral nervous system (PNS) is composed of all nerves that are moving impulses from the CNS to different areas of the body (this is how pain in sent. In our example, impulses move to a certain area to alert you to a problem with pain).

See Figure 3.1 PNS:

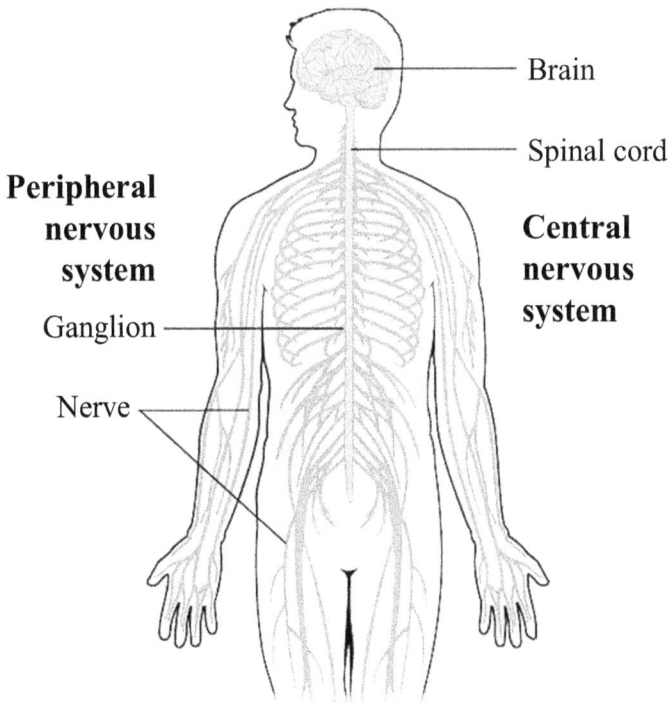

Figure 3.1 Central and Peripheral nervous systems

Lastly, a fast response (reflex, see Chapter 2) is caused when an action must be acted on (see figure 2.1) immediately. In an emergency, we do not even have time to study what is happening to us. In our example, the muscle would react very quickly to keep us from burning.

The body might respond with various actions. Some of these are sweating, heavy breathing, running, and all or some of our thoughts.

Note: If you are taught as a child to brush your teeth, it will become a permanent reflex over time. We treat these as habits.

Now, think about criminal activity as an example: Our laws are there to give us an idea of what is right or wrong. But, what is right or wrong depends on the situation. Law has been asking the question, why did someone commit a crime?

Remember nature versus nurture (see Chapter 1)?

From serious crimes to taking an extra apple, all involve the nervous system.

Take, for example, a man is on trial for murder. Is he innocent or guilty? What should be his punishment? If he is in an accident that caused brain damage as a child, does this play a part?

Defense argument: Brain damage made it impossible to make good decisions. He might be found not guilty, even though he did commit murder.

This has become one of the big problems in criminal trials for many years. We will look into this later.

CHAPTER 4

Neurotransmitters

Neurotransmitters are chemical molecules synthesized within the brain cells. They allow the transfer of signaling messages between the brain cells. The movement from nerve ending to nerve ending is controlled at the synapse (see Figure 4.1).

What do the brain chemicals do?

They are also called neurotransmitters; this word tells you all you need to know.

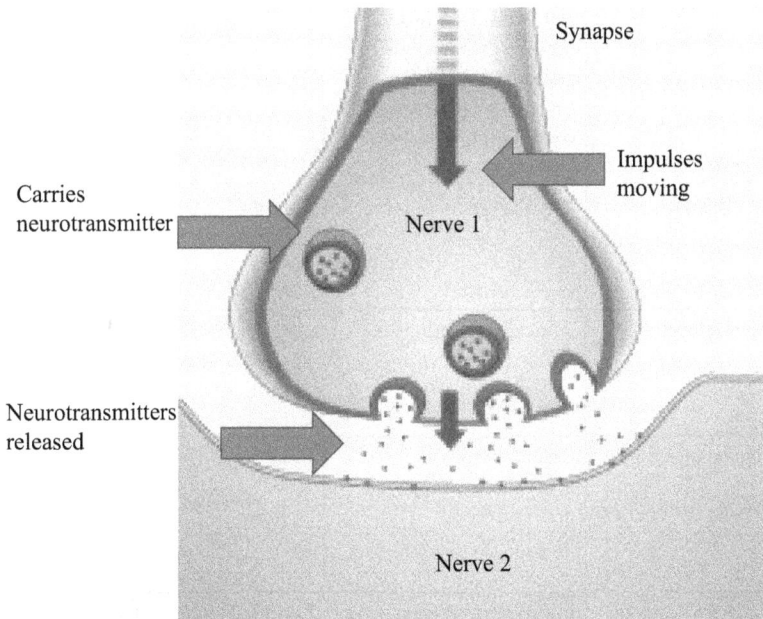

Figure 4.1 The impulses move through the synapse

Just separate the parts of the word: neuro (nerves) and transmitters (help the transition), and you can see that chemicals help impulses travel to the next neuron (see Figure 4.1).

Neurotransmitters all serve a different purpose in the brain and body. There are many of these, but we will pick out the major six: acetylcholine, dopamine, norepinephrine, serotonin, gamma-aminobutyric acid (more commonly referred to as GABA), and glutamate (see Table 4.1).

Questions

- What are the effects of release of these neurotransmitters? (see Table 4.1)

Table 4.1 Major neurotransmitters

Name	Purpose	Effect
Acetylcholine	Found throughout the nervous system. It is the only neurotransmitter that sends and receives information between the motor neurons and voluntary muscles (muscles you have conscious control over, such as the biceps).	Muscle stimulation Heart rate increase Sleep (avoid)
Dopamine	Regulates many aspects of behavior, including pleasure, emotion, and behavior (movements).	Learning Memory Mood Positive thinking
Norepinephrine	Also regulates behavior.	During stress, it ups the heart rate and courses the blood away from digestive systems to muscles. Called *fight or flight*.
Serotonin	Regulates mood and plays a major role in sleep, wakefulness, and eating.	Sleep Mood Appetite Pain Body temperature
GABA[1]* and glutamate	During stress, it helps us stay calm and not over-react.	Control during stressful situations (many be fixed with drugs).
Endorphins (three types)	When released, often during exercise, a rush of excitement and happy feelings result.	

*Gabapentin

- These neurotransmitters affect our behaviors and feelings (one example is a *runner's high* when exercise leaves you feeling happy).
- What is the effect of slow or no releases of neurotransmitters? Misconnection at the synapse, which makes it impossible for impulses to go on. Mutations in the genes that produce neurotransmitters are called synaptic malfunctions and have the same effect.

Many pharmaceuticals (prescription or street drugs) mimic neurotransmitters and have similar effects (example: cocaine and nicotine mimic endorphins).

Do you think pharmaceutical companies knew about this?

In addition to neurotransmitters, our brain is affected by the release of hormones from the sex organs; these hormones rise and fall during certain times.

Table 4.2 *Hormone*

Hormone	Who it affects	Increase of hormone occurs naturally	When hormones are released
Testosterone	Men**	Sex, anger, puberty, steroids	Violence, strength, may cause rage (steroids)
Estrogen	women***	Puberty, menstruation and pregnancy	Pregnancy and birth*

The two hormones in question here are estrogen (female) and testosterone (male).

**The sex hormone in men is testosterone, but men have estrogen too. High estrogenler in males can cause, infertility, erectile dysfunction and gycomastia (enlarged breasts).

***Women have both estrogen and testosterone. When the ovary cannot make estrogen (menopause), the estrogen stops, testosterone begins to become active. Symptoms might be, hair to grow on the face, Baldness, and other male secondary sex characteristics may show up.

*Estrogen increases when a woman is pregnant because the hormone is needed to keep the embryo in the uterus. When birth begins, estrogen drops significantly and the uterus expels its contents, this includes the fetus. If it is the time of birth contractions begin, Hormone levels come down after birth, due to a large drop last this time, and hormone fluxuation can cause a deep depression (post-partum depression), or worse, post-partum psychosis. Some mothers have killed their children (see chapter 10).

CHAPTER 5

How Might Genetics Change Behavior?

In a number of ways:

1. Chromosomal aberration (extra Y). See Figure 5.1
2. Single gene defects (caused by dominant or recessive genes). See Chapter 6.
3. Brain damage from injury or birth. See Table 5.1.
4. Epigenetic changes in the DNA itself during pregnancy caused by pollution and other environmental changes.

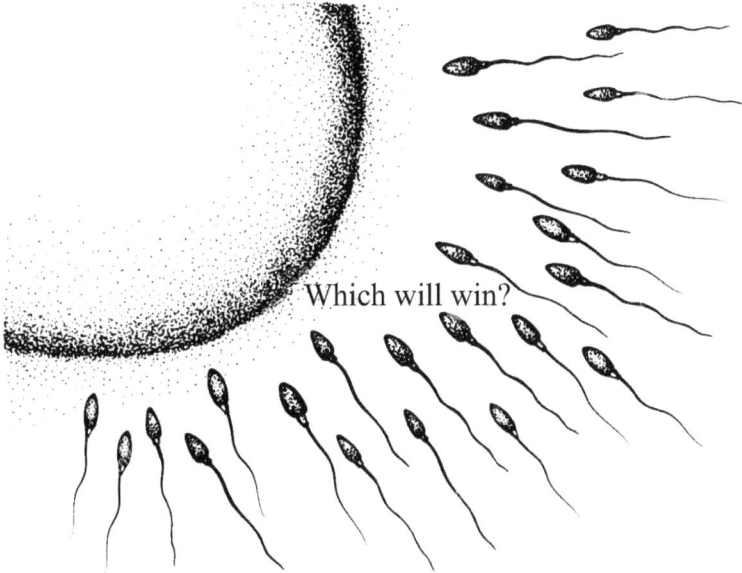

Which will win?

Figure 5.1 Sperm traveling to egg

Table 5.1 Genetic conditions that cause changes in behavior

Condition	How does this effect behavior	Symptoms	Diagnosis	Test	Treatment
Brain damage either before or after birth	Any problem during pregnancy or birth that causes brain damage.	Slow reflexes, cognitive skills later in life Deafness	Yes, before birth (amniocentesis) or in the first few months	Ultrasound before birth showing smaller brain size or damage	Physical therapy
Fragile X (broken X chromosome)	This happens during meiosis in the sperm or egg.	Mental retardation and explosive reactions	By taking cells from the fetus and testing a cell (amniocentesis)	Test for extra or a broken chromosome (amniocentesis)	Treat as they occur
Schizophrenia (inherited mental illness)	Shows up in late teens.	Behavioral problems, hallucinations Depression	Psychiatric help, institutional commitment and drugs	Diagnosis by analyzing behavior	Medication
Diabetes Diabetes 1 and 2	Extremes of blood sugar can affect behavior.	Dizziness, coma, hallucination, and if not corrected immediately, coma and death	Control of blood sugar with insulin injections or insulin pump	Type 1 is genetic and child is usually diagnosed early (very difficult to control) Type 2: Middle age, can be controlled with medications, diet, or insulin	Insulin, diet, and testing of blood
Chromosomal aberrations (see explanation next) ***	XXY XYY	Anger, violent behavior, hyperactivity, Learning	Amniocentesis and karyotyping. can be done in utero, and the disgnosis is given to the parents. They decide what action should be done.	No symptoms would show up at birth, determine this from a chromosome	Separate sperm and delete only Y bearing into the egg

***Think back to how a fetus' sex is determined.

Remember this??

X and Y are the two sex chromosomes.

Where do they come from? They are Formed in ovary and testes cells.

All eggs have an X

Sperm have *either* an X or Y.

Notice: This configuration means that when egg and sperm join, the egg *always* contributes X an. So, if you think about it—it is the male sperm that determines the sex. (If an X bearing sperm joins the egg—*It is a girl*! If a Y bearing sperm joins the egg—*It is a boy!*)

Sounds simple, right (see next). But, actually, *what* controls which sperm *joins* the egg?

If the couple wants a boy, is there anything they can do to make that happen?

How does an XYY configuration occur?

The Y chromosome creates the male hormone (testosterone) if two Ys exist in a fertilized egg; it seems obvious it might affect the testosterone levels in the fetus and the adult as well.

What causes this (XYY) to happen?

Actually, scientists are not sure, some have theorized (see Table 5.2).

Table 5.2 Theories

Theory 1	Two sperm join the egg	Yes, but under most circumstances, this would create a zygote with 69 chromosomes*.
Theory 2	Uneven meiosis causing chromosomes to stick together in sperm	During the process, chromosome pairs must separate.
Theory 3	Separation of Y chromosomes during meiosis	During the process, chromosome pairs must separate.
Theory 4	Sperm weight Lighter sperm swim faster? True?	Y bearing sperm have a chromosome (Y) that is half the size of X.
Theory 5	Father of this child also has an extra X in some sperm	Both the grandfather and father carry the extra Y. This can be determined by taking a sample from each.

Only embryos that carry the correction number will live

Most of these studied XYY men in prison for violent crimes. **

Year	Who studied?	Where done?	
1962	A male who had a Down syndrome child	Denmark	First patient tested.
1966	Richard Speck mass murderer (see Chapter 10)	First time brought up in a murder case	The testing was approved, but Speck did not have the extra Y.*
1970s		Patients in mental institutions con-victed of serious crimes Thinking was: XYY meant criminality	The feeling proved untrue.
1978–2006	Denmark	Long-term study did not involve any change in criminality	The risk of future conviction for those with XYY was slightly elevated.

*Speck's trial was covered heavily in the press, many thought if he tested positive for XYY it would prove his guilt, but he was XYY, and he was found guilty because of a witness.

*Many studies have been done and shown, but many still believe an extra Y means more testosterone and, therefore, more aggression.

Think about this: In the far future, all newborns will have to have their complete DNA sequence done. If the child's karyotype showed XYY, what might be done with this child?

CHAPTER 6

Does Any Single Gene Defect (Mutation) Cause Aggressiveness?

Could this be used as a defense in court?

What is monoamine oxidase A (MAOA) deficiency? Monoamine oxidase breaks down neurotransmitters (see figure 4.1) in the synapse, so when its gene is mutated, the next impulse would not continue through the synapse. This might cause changes in the behavior. Its gene is on the X chromosome; see Illustration 6.1.

Illustration 6.1 X chromosome with MAOA gene highlighted. See arrow

The following case is an interesting example of genetic testing and how it can affect a single case (and cases to come). Think about this as you read the following case: if the *cause* of Mobley's action and reaction was controlled by his mutated gene for MAOA deficiency, should his verdict reflect this?

*Mobley v Georgia***
455 S.E. 2nd 61 (1995)

Facts of the case:

On February 17, 1991, John Collins was shot in the back of the head. This occurred during a robbery of the Domino Pizza Store in Oakwood, CA.

He worked in Oakwood, CA, franchise. On March 13, after being picked up for questioning, Stephen Mobley confessed to murder and armed robbery.

During this confession, he boasted how John Collins fell on his knees and begged for mercy. Then, he had himself tattooed with a Domino's logo and plastered his cell with Domino's boxes. His history included rape, robbery, assault, and burglary. The prosecution said that "Mobley is evil, a cold blooded, heartless killer."

Daniel Summer, the court-appointed attorney for Mobley, tried to get a plea of guilty entered and a deal for life in prison, but, the deal was rejected. The court was interested in the death penalty for Mobley.

During questioning of Mobley's family, Summer met Joyce Ann Childers, his aunt. She told Summer that "volcanic, aggressive, physical abuse and violent behavior is prevalent throughout the family tree." Summer then remembered an article he had read in *The Chicago Tribune* in which scientists at Harvard, the National Institutes of Health (NIH), and labs overseas were conducting research on genetic ties to violence.

Before the sentencing hearing, Summer contacted the doctor from Harvard Medical School and another expert at Emory University**. When Mobley's story was revealed, the doctors began to see a pattern emerge of a family history of violence moving through a number of generations in Mobley's family (see Illustration 6.2). Both doctors offered their services free of charge, but Mobley would need specialized testing of urine and blood to determine if he suffers from a genetic mutation of the gene for MAOA, as the patients studied by Breakefield and Farat were.*

One might expect Mobley to come from poor family and bad surroundings, the opposite is actually true. Even though many of the people in Mobley's family tree were violent, many were amazingly successful. His father, for example, even though he refused to help Mobley's defense, is a self-made millionaire. He tried sending his son to private school, then psychiatrists, and finally, jail but stated, "He never developed a value system or a conscience." In the end, he washed his hands of the responsibility.

The cost of the tests, about 1,000 U.S. dollars, was not available to Mobley, and Summer asked the court to release funds for the test. This allowed the trial court, and eventually, the Supreme Court of Georgia, to weigh the question of validity of genetic causes of criminality.

Results: The Georgia trial court (the original court) found no reason for the test and did not release the money. In their decision, they stated: "the theory of a genetic connection is not at the level of scientific acceptance that would justify the release of the funds."

Pedigree of the Mobley family (see Figure 6.1).

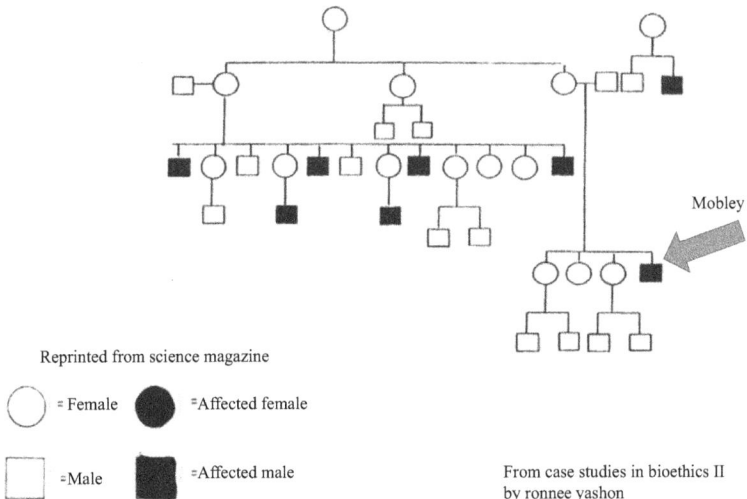

Reprinted from science magazine

◯ = Female   ● =Affected female

▢ =Male   ■ =Affected male

From case studies in bioethics II by ronnee yashon

Figure 6.1 What did you notice that only males are affected, arrow is Mobley? Gene mutated MAOA

CHAPTER 7

How Do We Study the Effects of Genetics on Behavior?

Well, if we could find two or more people with the exact same genetic code and compare their behaviors, we might find some differences.

But, who has the exact same genetic code?

Wait, identical twins do.

Nature versus nurture might be studied among twins separated at birth, and it has been.

Many studies analyzed individual questions such as: twins with different fathers, intelligence quotient (IQ), obesity, schizophrenia, homosexuality, and fingerprints.

The Number of twins, triplets, quadruplets are increasing. This is not because people are having twins in greater numbers but because of selective pregnancy. Also called assisted reproduction.

If a couple wants to have a baby they will need, as you already know, egg and sperm. In many infertility problems one or both of these important cells might be missing or in low numbers.

Doctors (called fertility doctors), women and men are asked to donate and when they come to the clinic, they are paid for this donation. The sperm and egg are then frozen and when they are needed, they are thawed, then fertilized in the lab and placed inside a woman. There might be many eggs made by the donors and if the woman wants to have more than one placed in her uterus. Should we be doing this? I'm afraid it's already been done at a very large scale.

PS identical twins cannot be formed from this method, only fraternal twins

Lets review how Identical twins occur. I am sure you remember that have identical DNA. If you have known any, it is sometimes hard to tell them apart.

They are formed from ONE fertilized egg that splits into two embryos,

Most people think that they are EXACT. But as time goes by things (DNA), might change.

When a woman ovulates she "usually" gives off one egg, it is then fertilized by sperm

Go back and look at figure 8.1 and be amazed!

Usually fertilized egg splits ONCE but how did the egg split 5 times?

The Number of twins, triplets, quadruplets are increasing. This is not because people are having twins in greater numbers but because of selective pregnancy. Also called assisted reproduction.

If a couple wants to have a baby they will need, as you already know, egg and sperm. In many infertility problems one or both of these important cells might be missing or in low numbers.

Doctors (called fertility doctors)This isn't as bad as it sounds, women and men are asked to donate and when they come to the clinic, they are paid for this many eggs made by the donors and if the woman wants to have more than one placed in donation. The sperm and egg are then frozen and when they are needed, they are thawed, then fertilized in the lab and placed inside a woman.   ;done at a very large scale.

Identical twins cannot be formed from this method, only fraternal twins.

An example: Documentary called "Identical Strangers"

Story: triplets were born to a woman, who gave them up for adoption through a local placement service.

When they arrived at the service, a comment was made that putting them in different homes might make an interesting study.

Research was done and three very different families were selected and were never told the other two existed. For years, after the placement the children were studied, but nothing was ever published.

It was discovered when one of the triplets enrolled in junior college. As he walking to registration, a few people hugged him and said they were glad he was back. As he was getting over his surprise a student came up and said, "do you have a twin? I have a friend who looks just like you. Let's call him."

Available on amazon An example: Documentary called "Identical Strangers"

Story: triplets were born to a woman, who gave them up for adoption through a local placement service.

When they arrived at the service, a comment was made that putting them in different homes might make an interesting study.

Research was done and three very different families were selected and were never told the other two existed. For years, after the placement the children were studied, but nothing was ever published.

It was discovered when one of the triplets enrolled in junior college. As he walking to registration, a few people hugged him and said they were glad he was back. As he was getting over his surprise a student came up and said, "do you have a twin? I have a friend who looks just like you. Let's call him."

Available on amazon (its worth seeing)

EPIGENETICS

Why do identical twins have differences at all? Not just in health outcomes, but temperament, taste and physical traits can be traced back to how each siblings' genes are expressed . These microscopic variations can lead to radical differences in the twins. The study of how this works it's called epigenetics. In this scenario, changes are microscopic and are difficult to identify.

Scientists are actively working on the specific things that the epigenome can do. Their main function is to turn on and off genes as needed. Certain parts of the genome need to be turned on before the gene can function and this is what the epigenome does.

One example might be a gene is in the eye that is making too many tears, it should do its job normally but the epigenome may have another idea, it activates another DNA strand to turn this gene Off.

Other things that affect the epigenome are environmental changes, disease and flaws.

Scientists are working to find the exact part of the genome that's each epigenome affects. This might be involved with aging, the ability to do strenuous work and intelligence.

Some scientists would like to find out how to turn on or off some genes to enhance humans for the for future or cure a genetic disease.

Have any ideas for a Sci-Fi movie?

FAUX case: When they were born, Mark and Mike looked so alike their mother couldn't tell them apart. And their eyes were strikingly BLUE. As they got older, they carefully looked for differences all the time (each wanted be independent). When they were in college, Mark was noticing his left eye had gotten darker. In the next year, it became dark brown.

The other stayed blue.

Is the culprit epigenetics?

CHAPTER 8

Twin Studies

Twin studies have been going on for many years; even then, we had no clue about how complex twins can be. Many scientists made observations, and so did the parents of twins. As you already figured out, there are two types of twins: monozygotic (identical) twins and heterozygotic twins (two different egg and sperm fuse). We talked about what a perfect scientific study they would be. They might teach us something.

Note: With the development of assisted reproduction, many more multiple births (triplets, quads, quintuplets, and more) have happened because when an embryo is produced and the mother wants to implant (two or more frozen embryos), the doctor usually inserts a number of embryos (1–5), and then, they wait.

Twins reared-apart studies have certainly helped generate some interesting hypotheses, but they have completely failed to provide scientifically acceptable evidence in support of genetic influences on human behavioral differences, which include intelligence quotient (IQ), personality, and psychiatric disorders. It has been acknowledged in 2014, "In spite of numerous studies with sufficient power to detect rather small effects," the results of attempts to uncover genes for general intelligence (*g*) have been dismal in comparison with expectation.

Figure 8.1. The most famous identical quintuplets: Dionne Quints

Believe it or not: One fertilized egg splits five times.
Their story:

- Born in backwoods of Canada
- A midwife thought they would not live and placed them near the fire
- A doctor came to see them and said, "I will raise them"

For 25 years, they lived with him and his nurses. He built a house with a large window all around and charged people to come and watch them play, eat, and open presents.

They never saw their parents until they were teens.

Other Important studies:

The Two Jims (famous case in all biology books)

In 1979, Jim Springer and Jim Lewis, *the Jim twins*, were reunited at age 39 after not knowing the other existed. As described in Segal's book on the identical Jim twins, *Born Together—Reared Apart*, both had been adopted and raised by different families in Ohio, just 40 miles apart from each other. Despite their separate upbringings, it turned out that both twins got terrible migraines, bit their nails, smoked Salem cigarettes, drove light-blue Chevrolets, did poorly in spelling and math, and had worked at McDonald's and as part-time deputy sheriffs. But, the weirdest part was that one of the Jim twins had named his first son James Alan. The other had named his first son James Allan. Both had named their pet dogs Toy. Both had also married women named Linda; then, they got divorced, and both married women named Betty.

Is this possible?

A few other cases:

Two girls adopted in China by two American families did not find each other until high school. They lived in separate cities, but were bought together by a friend who was shopping and saw a twin of her friend.

Later, they traveled together to China and met their birth mother.

"There are some twins in Brazil, where one twin has microcephaly due to the Zika virus infection and the does other not," he adds. "And you'd really think, 'Hold on a minute, how does that happen if the mother gets infected, why does only one twin get infected?'" As a recent study on twins exposed to Zika in pregnancy suggested, infection risk could be related to epigenetic mechanisms.

Two of the identical twins raised apart (Jorge and William) shared the same bump on the same spot on the bridge of their nose, and until they were reunited, both had been convinced that it was from an injury. They also both preferred only eating the drumsticks of chicken. But, one wore glasses, and the other did not. The other identical pair (Carlos and Wilber) had both been smokers, and both had a speech impediment.

CHAPTER 9

Legal and Ethical Questions

Speaking of mashups ... the four areas shown in the normally just slightly touch each other, but today, however, science is being smothered by each of them.

Example: Global warming

In the topic of this book, we run into a kind of collision (legal actions, divorce, murder, and of course, law) and ethics are separate topics, but

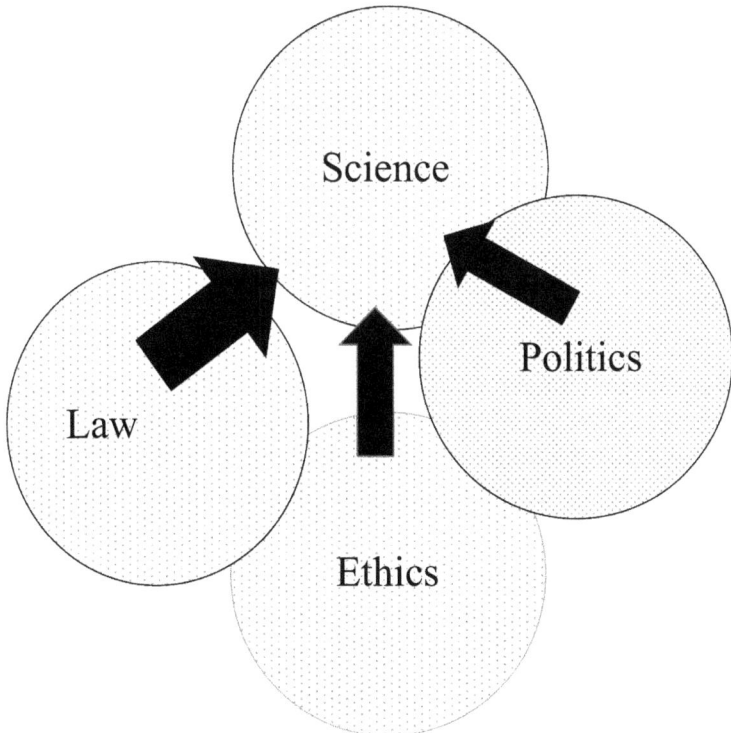

Figure 9.1 Mashup

because this not only is *nature versus nurture*, the discussion of the two are a mashup and show up in some odd areas. How should we raise our children? Is there a difference in the way we, as parents, act because of how grew up or our genetics? This messes with legal verdicts in a court of law (some serious, some not). How do these questions sound to you?

Are parents libel for what their children do?

If a person has committed a serious crime

and is a teen should they be punished?

Example: This year, we have been exposed to a few examples, one of the most interesting is a parent or child mashup.

The college admission scandal. Parents (well-known people) paid large amounts to get their child into colleges.

HUMAN BEHAVIOR MULTIPLE CHOICE QUESTION 6

Related to the preceding case

a. *The parents should be punished*

b. *Only the parents and the universities should be punished*

c. *The children should be punished*

d. *None of the above*

e. *A and B*

f. *Only A*

Answers:

a. *The parents got jail time and huge fines, but is that enough?*

b. *Universities must have people spearheading this kind of scam.*

c. *Did the children have a part in this?*

d. *No one? Why could this not happen?*

Note: The children are *not* enrolled at this time, did the universities drop them because of the scandal? Should they be punished?

Case	Ethical question	Genetics	Law	Outcome
University scandal	Why did the parents do this?	Were the parents assuming their child would not get in?	Were the children part of this?	Parents held responsible
As a teen, a child steals from a store.	Is this the parent's fault?	Why did they steal?	Who was harmed?	Maybe no one?
As an adult, the child commits a larger crime	Serious ones	Possibly, but even testing how to prove it	But, are we ready to accept such punishment?	Depends on the age
Are parents *ever* responsible?	Their influence?	There have been some cases?	This is nature versus nurture.*	Example: School shootings

Should any of these things be taken into consideration in a trial?

The defendant's age? Been proven due to scans of brains and studies of young and old.
The defendant's childhood? It is not necessary that we\ blame the family but the pedigrees could be used?
His/her parents' treatment? Does this cause brain damage?

Can we ever say that a reaction is completely controlled by genetics. If the answer is YES, no one would be responsible for their actions. Also if genes control what behaviors we have, then, we are probably NOT responsible. If we do an action that is triggered by genetics some questions arise:

a. *Can we control everything we do?*
b. *If we cannot control a behavior, how can this lead to a guilty verdict?*
c. *If we can control our actions, why didn't we*
d. *Often when asked why a person did something, they say "I don't know, I was drunk." Are we responsible for our actions if we were drinking?*

Humans want to believe that we are responsible for what we do! But are we?

BUT MANY PEOPLE TRY TO DEFEND THEMSELVES BY ARGUING THEY HAD A SERIOUSLY BAD CHILDHOOD. THEY WERE BEATEN, MOLESTED, IGNORED AND LIVED IN MANY FOSTER HOMES, ETC. (is this possible?)

CHAPTER 10

Famous or Infamous Cases

In the law and in actual life, we judge a person's behavior with our own moral code. But, in a court of law, there are more restrictions and controversy.

Each of these cases has been about how our brain and its memories and genetics applies to the reason for behaviors. As scientific to study of DNA, genes, brain chemicals, and age (brain size) continues to gather information, it is an application the can apply actual cases.

	Name of case	Type of crime		Actual question	Background
	FRYE versus USA Used to decide what was 'REAL' science and what was not. The FRYE questions applied to each science were: 1. To which scientific field does the evidence or testimony belong? 2. Is the evidence or testimony generally accepted in this field? 3. What constitutes general acceptance? How do you think these questions are holding up with today's science?	Use of lie detector as evidence		Should lie detector results be used as evidence	In his book, The Truth Machine, James Halperin envisions a future with a machine that can determine lying with no error. What effect do you think this would have on courtrooms?
1	Hinkley versus USA (October 09, 1980)	Assassination attempt of Ronald Reagan and wounded James Brady	Found not guilty by reason of insanity and spent many years in a mental hospital	Was Hinkley insane? Eventually, he was released to live with his mother in 2018.	Because he was in love with Jodie Foster, he shot at Reagan to get her attention; movie connection
2	Andrea Yates	Drowned all her children in the bathtub	She had just given birth	Is post-partum depression insanity?	Many thought no one could be sane and do this

3	Roper versus Simmons	With three of his friends, they pushed a woman from a railroad trestle	Simmons was 16	Should a juvenile be tried as an adult?	Brain chemicals? Brain damage? Just a teenager?
4	Richard Speck	Killed three student nurses in their apartment, but left a witness	I lived in Chicago, watched TV showing the police carried body bags out. after	Was he mentally ill?	He killed all, but one, who hid under the bed and escaped. Later, she testified
5	John Wayne Gacy	Murdered many boys in Chicago	Picked them up, killed them, and buried them in his basement	He and his wife lived in the home until he was caught	He worked at children's parties dressed like a clown
	Other legal theories based on behavior				
	Battered wife syndrome	For years, women who were beaten by their husbands were blamed if they fought back	First case	The most famous case was made into a TV movie called the Burning bed. It was based on a case in Michigan in 1977, Many of these cases went before a jury who found her "not guilty". It was appealed to the appellate court and overturned.	
	Use of steroids athlete violence	Think about the number of athletes harmed or killed their wives	Cases: *People versus Simpson*	There are many cases of men being abusive and sometimes killing girlfriend Or wife. No one presented this defense in the OJ trial but it was known he used.	

Interesting addendum

As you have seen, it is not clear what wins the *nature versus nurture* argument, but think about this:

Since the beginning of the era of assisted reproduction, things have changed quite a bit. Problems with infertility in both men and women have brought to light the following:

- Sperm counts in men are decreasing.
- Women are waiting longer to have children.
- How this research changed my thinking.../
- If the infertility continues the world will definitely change.
  There have been many movies looking to the future.
- Some are: The Handmaids tale

What does it seem we need? Sperm and egg donors.

In the past, we have picked out mates by geography* (not too much travel), but as all society changed ... we could not find mates.

So, clinics began to cater to men and women who were infertile and began collecting samples of sperm and eggs stored the frozen gametes and embryos to help. *But, this was* not free!

Which sperm or egg donor would you choose?

Sperm and egg *banks* took long family and genetics histories (diseases, personality, criminal record as well as beauty, eye color, intelligence). Some sperm banks even offer look-alikes (Brad Pitt).

People would want what they want!

Remember the mashup: Can this affect what kind of child they create, and if we look ahead, narrow our choices?

Bibliography

M.R. Cummings. 2017. *Human Heredity*.

Contributing Writers, Genetic Literacy Project

Jack El-Hai. 2016. *XYY Men.*

Laura, F. July 21, 2017. "What is Psychoneuroplasticity?" *Originsrecovery.com.*

Erika, H. May15, 2018. *Identical Twins Hint at Environments Change Gene Expression.* The Atlantic.

Elysium, H. September 13, 2018. "The Science of Twins and How it Settled the Nature v. Nurture Debate." Endpoints.elysiumhealth.com.

Nancy, S. 2018. "Born Together, Reared Apart." Indiebound.org

Tim, W. (director). 2018. "Three Identical Strangers." *Documentary.*

R. Yashon. June 18, 2012. *Landmark Legal Cases in Science,* 5th ed.

2014. *RJ Publications.*

Yashon, R., and M.R. Cummings. 2015. *Human Genetics and Society, 2nd ed.* Cengage Learning.

About the Authors

Ronnee Yashon is a nationally known expert in teaching genetics, ethics, and the law on all levels. She has a background in teaching in the high school, undergraduate, graduate, and law school levels.

Her case study methodology for introducing bioethics and law, uses simple, personalized, and current scenarios that involve the students in decision making.

Michael R. Cummings is the author or coauthor of several college textbooks, including Human Heredity Principles and Issues, Concepts of Genetics, and Essentials of Genetics. He was a faculty member at the University of Illinois at Chicago for over 25 years.

Today, Mike teaches general biology, cell biology, and genetics at the Illinois Institute of Technology.

Index

acetylcholine, v, 10
amazon, 23
assisted reproduction, 21
autonomic reflex, 3

behavior
    defined, 1
    genetic conditions causing changes
        in, 13–16
    genetic effects on, 21–23
    nature *versus* nurture, ix, 1
Born Together—Reared Apart (Segal),
    26
brain
    areas of, 5
    functions, 3–4
    damage, 8, 13

central nervous system (CNS), 7
The Chicago Tribune, 18
chromosomal aberration, 13

DNA, 13, 16, 22, 23
dopamine, v, 10
drug testing, animal *versus* human
    in, 2

endorphin, v
epigenetics, 23–24
estrogen (female), 11–12

fertility doctors, 21, 22
fraternal twins, 22

gamma-aminobutyric acid (GABA),
    10
genetic conditions
    behavior changes and, 13–16
    sex hormones and, 15
    theories about, 15
    XYY and, 16

genetic testing cases, 18–19
genetics
    legal and ethical questions, 29–32
    legal cases, 33–36
    twin studies in, 25–27
global warming, 29–30
glutamate, 10

heterozygotic twins (two different egg
    and sperm fuse), 25
hormones, 11–12
    sex, 15
human brain. *See* brain

Identical Strangers (documentary), 23
identical twins, 22
intelligence quotient (IQ), 21, 25

Jim twins, The (Springer and Lewis), 26

legal and ethical questions in genetics,
    29–32
Lewis, Jim, 26

Mobley v Georgia, 18–19
monoamine oxidase A (MAOA)
    deficiency, 17–19
monozygotic (identical) twins, 25
mutation, 17–19

neurotransmitters, 9–11, 17
    effects of release of, 10
norepinephrine, v, 10

peripheral nervous system (PNS), 7

reflex arc, 4
reflex(es)
    autonomic, 3
    other, 3
    somatic, 3

Segal, Nancy L., 26
serotonin, v, 10
sex hormones, 15
single gene defect, 17–19
somatic reflex, 3
Springer, Jim, 26
synapse, 4, 9, 11, 17

testosterone (male), 11–12, 15

twin studies, 25–27
    types of, 25

X chromosome, 15, 17
XYY, 15–16

Y chromosome, 15

Zika virus, 27

OTHER TITLES IN OUR HUMAN GENETICS AND SOCIETY COLLECTION

Ronnee Yashon, Editor

Human Genetics and the Immune System
by Ronnee Yashon and Michael R. Cummings

DNA Forensics
by Ronnee Yashon and Michael R. Cummings

Biotechnology
by Ronnee Yashon and Michael R. Cummings

Chromosomes
by Ronnee Yashon and Michael R. Cummings

Genetic Testing
by Ronnee Yashon and Michael R. Cummings

Fertility, Infertility, and Treatment Options
by Ronnee Yashon and Michael R. Cummings

Announcing Digital Content Crafted by Librarians

Momentum Press offers digital content as authoritative treatments of advanced engineering topics by leaders in their field. Hosted on ebrary, MP provides practitioners, researchers, faculty, and students in engineering, science, and industry with innovative electronic content in sensors and controls engineering, advanced energy engineering, manufacturing, and materials science.

Momentum Press offers library-friendly terms:

- perpetual access for a one-time fee
- no subscriptions or access fees required
- unlimited concurrent usage permitted
- downloadable PDFs provided
- free MARC records included
- free trials

The **Momentum Press** digital library is very affordable, with no obligation to buy in future years.

For more information, please visit **www.momentumpress.net/library**

www.ingramcontent.com/pod-product-compliance
Lightning Source LLC
Chambersburg PA
CBHW060514220326
41598CB00025B/3649